Adventures in Canadian History

STEEL ACROSS THE PLAINS

PIERRE BERTON

STEEL ACROSS
THE PLAINS

ILLUSTRATIONS BY PAUL MCCUSKER

M&S

An M&S Paperback Original from
McClelland & Stewart Inc.
The Canadian Publishers

An M&S Paperback Original from McClelland & Stewart Inc.

First printing September 1992

Canadian Cataloguing in Publication Data

Berton, Pierre, 1920-
Steel across the plains

(Adventures in Canadian history. Canada moves west)
"An M&S paperback original."
Includes index.
ISBN 0-7710-1441-4

1. Canadian Pacific Railway Company – History – Juvenile literature.
2. Railroads – Prairie Provinces – History – Juvenile literature.   3. Van Horne,
William Cornelius, Sir, 1843-1915 – Juvenile literature.   4. Canadian Pacific
Railway Company – Biography – Juvenile literature.   5. Businessmen –
Canada – Biography – Juvenile literature.   I. McCusker, Paul.   II. Title.
III. Series: Berton, Pierre, 1920-   . Adventures in Canadian history. Canada
moves west.

HE2810.C3B4 1992   j385′.09712   C92-093706-3

Series cover design by Tania Craan
Cover design by Stephen Kenny
Cover illustration by Scott Cameron
Interior illustrations by Paul McCusker
Maps by James Loates
Editor: Peter Carver

Typesetting by M&S

Printed and bound in Canada

McClelland & Stewart Inc.
The Canadian Publishers
481 University Avenue
Toronto, Ontario
M5G 2E9

Contents

Maps appear on pages 12, 62, and 85.

The events in this book actually happened as told here. Nothing has been made up. This is a work of non-fiction and there is archival evidence for every story and, indeed, every remark made in this book.

Adventures in Canadian History

STEEL ACROSS THE PLAINS

OVERVIEW

The shape of the nation

CANADA IS DECEPTIVELY VAST. The map shows it as the largest country in the world and probably the greatest in depth from north to south. It is almost twice as deep as the United States and much deeper than either China or Russia.

But that is an illusion. For practical purposes Canada is almost as slender as Chile. Half its people live within a hundred miles (160 km) of the U.S. border, ninety percent of them within two hundred miles (320 km). It is a country shaped like a river or a railway, and for the best of reasons. In the eastern half of the nation this horizontal bunching of the population is due to the presence of the St. Lawrence River, in the western half to the Canadian Pacific Railway.

More than most countries, Canada owes its existence to its transcontinental railways. It was the promise of a railway to the Pacific that brought British Columbia into Confederation. It was the presence of that railway – the Canadian Pacific – that brought one million immigrants to the Canadian prairies at the turn of the century.

The American symbol of western expansion is the covered wagon. The Canadian symbol is the CPR colonist car. Every country has in its background a great national moment – a revolution, a military victory, a civil war. Ours is the building of a railway. The Trans-Canada Highway, which follows the railway route, is a continuation of that effort to tie the country together.

The CPR was the natural extension of the route used by explorers and fur traders in their passage to the Northwest. If that natural extension had been continued as was originally planned, Canada might today have a different shape. But in the spring of 1881 a handful of men gathered around a cluttered circular table in an office in St. Paul, Minnesota, and altered the shape and condition of the new country west of Winnipeg.

That decision affected the lives of tens of thousands of Canadians. It created a new network of cities close to the border that might not have existed for another generation, if ever – Broadview, Regina, Moose Jaw, Swift Current, Medicine Hat, Calgary, Banff, and Revelstoke.

It doomed others – Carlton, Battleford, Eagle Hill, Bethlehem, Grenoble, Baldwin, Humboldt, Nazareth, Nut Hill.

It affected aspects of Canadian life as varied as the tourist trade and the wheat trade. And it gave the CPR something very close to absolute control over the future of scores of new communities along the line of the railway.

That was not what the government had originally

intended when it began planning the railway in 1871, or even in 1881 when the job was taken over by a private company. The original route led northwest, away from the U.S. border, along the old Carlton Trail in the wooded valleys of the North Saskatchewan River. The three directors of the Canadian Pacific – George Stephen, the president, Richard Angus, and James Jerome Hill – decided to run the line south as close to the border as possible.

They had their reasons. They wanted to go through land that had not been settled so that they could control the real estate around their own railway stations. In this way they could prevent real estate speculators from making all the profits on the land. These people bought land cheaply in the belief that the railway would cross it. Then they could sell it to the CPR for much more than they had paid.

The CPR abandoned the careful route that government surveyors had explored and laid out in the previous decade at great cost in life, hardship, and expense (see *The Railway Pathfinders*). It would be another thirty years before that original route would be used by another railway – the Canadian Northern – now a part of the Canadian National Railway system.

The CPR's directors were encouraged by a bright-eyed amateur botanist named John Macoun. He had visited the so-called Palliser Triangle in the southern prairies in a particularly wet season. He told the three directors, quite wrongly, that there would be no problems for future farmers.

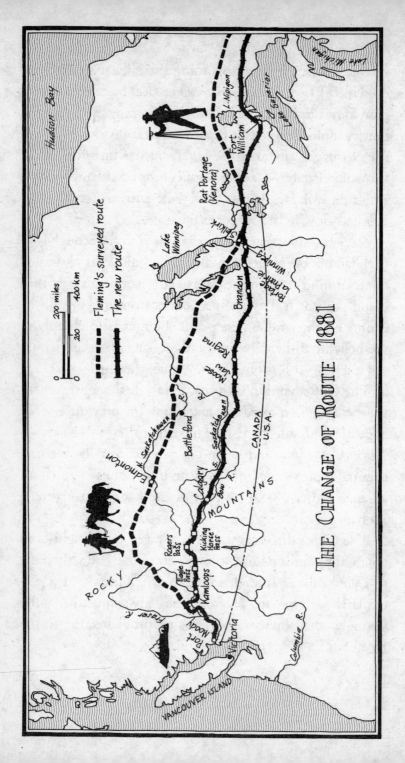

The Change of Route 1881

Hudson Bay

Lake Michigan

L. Nipigon

Fort William

L. Superior

Rat Portage (Kenora)

Lake Winnipeg

Selkirk

Winnipeg

Portage la Prairie

Brandon

200 miles
400 km
200

Fleming's surveyed route

The new route

Regina

Moose Jaw

N. Saskatchewan R.

Battleford

S. Saskatchewan R.

Edmonton

Calgary

Bow R.

CANADA

U.S.A.

ROCKY

Rogers Pass

Eagle Pass

Kicking Horse Pass

MOUNTAINS

Kamloops

Fraser R.

Port Moody

Victoria

VANCOUVER ISLAND

Columbia R.

The Palliser Triangle is a continuation of the Great American Desert. It has its wet years, and as every farmer now knows it has its dry years when almost nothing will grow without irrigation. But Macoun didn't know about the dry years. The railway builders took him at his word, and so the route of the CPR was changed, and the whole structure of the Canadian West was changed with it.

CHAPTER ONE

~

The birth of Brandon

JOHN MCVICAR WAS CERTAIN HE was going to be rich. His farm at Grand Valley, Manitoba, lay directly in the path of the new Canadian Pacific Railway which had been formed in 1880. Now, in the spring of 1881, McVicar was expecting an offer for his farm in Grand Valley. He was about to be bitterly disappointed.

Railway lines, like the CPR, are cut up into divisions, just as provinces are cut up into townships or counties. The little settlement of Grand Valley lay clustered on the banks of the Assiniboine River about 130 miles (208 km) west of Winnipeg. McVicar realized that the first divisional point on the prairie line after Winnipeg would have to be established right on his farm. It would become a headquarters for trainmen, conductors and railway workers. Marshalling yards would spring up, and freight and passenger cars would be shunted about to make up new trains. Supplies would pour in and so would settlers. Grand Valley would become a big community.

McVicar increased the size of his house, doubled the

capacity of his warehouse, and waited for an offer. It came quickly that April from the Canadian Pacific Railway's chief surveyor, General Thomas Lafayette Rosser, a tall Virginian who had fought on the Southern side in the American Civil War (1861-65). Rosser offered him $50,000.

John McVicar was about to take the money when his friends urged him to hold out for more. He asked Rosser for $60,000 – a big mistake. Rosser turned on his heel. "I'll be damned if a town of any kind is built here," he said.

He ordered his horse saddled, crossed the Assiniboine River and made straight for the shack of D.H. Adamson. He bought Adamson's property for a fraction of the price he'd offered McVicar. That was the end of Grand Valley, and the beginning of the new town of Brandon.

The railway wouldn't bargain with anybody. It simply moved its Grand Valley station two miles (3.2 km) further west into the Brandon Hills. That would be the CPR's method for all future dealings when private citizens tried to hold it up.

The new town was born on May 9, 1881. That was the day on which a Winnipeg surveyor arrived to subdivide it into avenues, streets, blocks, and lots. The main street was named after General Rosser, who insisted the lots be small so more money could be made. The survey took until mid-August, but the lots went on sale long before it was finished. Once the location of the new town was known, people began to appear and tents blossomed all along the high bank of the Assiniboine.

James Canning arrives at the "paper town" of Brandon, Manitoba.

When it became clear that Grand Valley was dying, its leading grocery store moved to Brandon. It was floated in sections by barge to the new townsite. By June two more stores and a billiard hall had also moved to Brandon. The CPR's clear intention was to destroy Grand Valley as a community.

Lots on both townsites went on sale at the end of May. A brief advertisement proclaimed that "McVicar's Landing" was a CPR crossing. But the name of the new town of Brandon first appeared May 30. Brandon lots sold at prices that ranged from $63 to $355. Grand Valley lots went badly and sold for an average of $33. The original community was clearly doomed.

The first newcomers had difficulty finding the new Brandon. James Canning trudged across the prairie looking for work. He arrived at the corner of 10th and Rosser and asked a man where the town was.

"Right here," came the reply.

Canning looked about him. There was only one other building in sight. "I don't see any town," Canning said.

"Well, it's only a paper town yet," his acquaintance replied.

The paper town blossomed swiftly into a tent community. The first post office was nothing more than a soap box with a slit for mail placed outside a tent. The first restaurant was a plank laid across two barrels on the trail that was to become Pacific Avenue. The first church services were held out of doors in a driving rain storm that June. The local harness maker held an umbrella over the minister's head while the congregation, composed entirely of young men, sang lustily in spite of the downpour.

In that golden summer of 1881, the pattern of the new Canada began to take hesitant shape along the line of the railway. Brandon was the beginning – the first of the scores of raw communities that would erupt from the naked prairie. Its birth pangs would be repeated again and again as the rails moved west. There was a kind of an electric feeling in the atmosphere – a sense of being in on the start of a great adventure – that the newcomers who arrived that summer would never forget.

In future years when other memories became blurred, those early pioneers would always keep the bright memory of those first months when the sharp, spring air was ripe with the scent of fresh lumber and ringing with the noise of construction; when lasting friendships began among the soiled tents on the riverbank; when every man was young and strong and in love with life; and when the distant prairie, unmarked by shovel or plough, was still a mysterious realm waiting to be claimed.

For those who planned to stay, the opportunities were almost unlimited. Of the first seven lawyers who arrived, four became cabinet ministers and a fifth Leader of the Opposition in the Manitoba legislature. The first organist in the church became the mayor of the city four times running. From grading the bumps on Sixth Street, Douglas Cameron rose to be Lieutenant-Governor of Manitoba.

A jovial young Irish ploughman from Ontario named Pat Burns went on to become the meat packing king of the Canadian West.

By August the town had acquired a dozen frame buildings, including two hotels. On October 11 the first passenger train pulled into the station and a boom of epic proportions was in full swing. The coming of the railway was transforming the west and the changes were spectacular enough to set the continent buzzing. But Grand Valley lapsed into decay. John McVicar and his brother, Dugald, tried to sell their townsite and failed. In the end they took $1,500 for it.

One man passing through early in '82 described Grand Valley as "a living corpse. The few buildings were forlorn. The business that was still being done … made a noise like a death rattle. The CPR had refused to stop trains there."

Some years later a surveyor named Charles Shaw came upon John McVicar ploughing in the vicinity with a team of mules. The farmer ran out onto the road. "Oh Mr. Shaw, I was a damn fool. If I'd only taken your advice, I would have been well off now!" For future speculators the fate of the little community on the Assiniboine was an object lesson in how not to deal with the railway.

William Cornelius Van Horne, the brilliant general manager of the CPR.

CHAPTER TWO

The Railway General

WILLIAM CORNELIUS VAN HORNE was made the CPR's general manager in January of 1882. When he announced that he would build five hundred miles (800 km) of track across the empty plains in a single season, very few people believed him. The whole prairie country from Brandon to the Rockies was virtually empty of people, except for bands of roving Indians and a few trappers and fur traders.

There were no roads, no bridges, and no trees. To build five hundred miles of steel in a single summer, the new-formed Canadian Pacific Railway company would have to bring every scrap of timber for bridges, railway ties, and buildings from hundreds of miles away. They would also have to bring in steel rails, bridging material, food for the employees, work tools and giant scrapers – all on rails as the line of steel was constructed. Only a man of Van Horne's determination could even consider such a thing.

The Canadian Pacific Railway company was a brand-new organization only a year old. The job of this private firm was to construct a line of steel all the way from North Bay on Lake Nipissing, in Ontario, to the Eagle Pass in the Gold Range of British Columbia. The government contractor would finish the line to the west coast. The government had also tried to build a railway across the Canadian shield in Northern Ontario, without much luck. The new CPR company was hired to finish that job. But its first task was to open up the prairies.

The CPR directors wanted that done as quickly as possible. They had been given ten years to finish the railway, but they were planning to complete it in a much shorter time. It was absolutely necessary to get the whole line into operation as quickly as possible, because they knew that for many years there would be very little local traffic.

It was the transcontinental trade that counted. A cargo such as silk demanded speedy transport, for silk is perishable. The CPR would have an advantage over its United States rivals because its route was much shorter. The coast of British Columbia was closer to the Orient than that of California. But the railway couldn't turn a dollar of profit until the last spike was driven.

Among railwaymen south of the border, Van Horne had a reputation for doctoring sick railroads until they were made to pay. He was also known as a fighter who had battled grasshoppers, labour unions, and other railways. Up to this point he had always won.

He told the CPR directors in Montreal that he could lay five hundred miles of prairie line in one year – an announcement that was greeted with skepticism. As one man said, "It was a feat unparalleled in railway history." A previous manager hadn't been able to lay more than 130 miles (208 km) of track in a single year, and here was Van Horne offering to quadruple that.

Still, this new man seemed to know a terrifying amount about railroading. He knew all about yards and repair shops. He understood the mysteries of accounting. He could work out a complicated system of scheduling in his head, while others sweated with pins and charts. He could understand the chatter of a telegraph key. He could operate any locomotive built. He even redesigned railway stations to his own taste. He was a product of his times – there is no one quite like him in today's business community.

He was probably one of the most engaging and versatile immigrants that this country has ever attracted across its borders – cheerful, capable, ingenious, temperamental, blunt, forceful, boyish, self-reliant, imaginative, hard-working, mischievous, and courageous. All those adjectives apply, but the one that sums him up best is the word "positive." As J.H.E. Secretan, his chief surveyor, said, " The word 'cannot' did not exist in his dictionary."

If he knew failure, he never showed it. Nor did he ever show any emotion behind the grave mask of his face or his penetrating blue eyes. He believed in coming to the point swiftly with the fewest possible words. It was the same with railway lines. The best run lines he knew were the ones that reached their destination with the shortest number of miles. And so one of his first jobs was to make sure the CPR would reach the Pacific Ocean by the shortest possible route.

His first decision – on January 13, 1882 – was to change the point at which the road entered the Rockies. Several of the passes in the mountains had already been surveyed. One, the Yellowhead, had been chosen by the chief engineer of Canada, Sir Sandford Fleming. But Van Horne felt it was too far north.

The CPR chose the Kicking Horse Pass, well to the south, not far from the present site of Calgary. This pass had not been surveyed but Van Horne was sure it would work. So here he was, proposing to drive steel directly across the plains at the mountain barrier without knowing exactly how to get through.

He had been hired as general manager of the CPR; someday he would be president. A man of great ambition, his love of power had its roots in his childhood and youth. He had started out as a telegraph operator. When he was eighteen, he was struck by the sight of the general superintendent of the Michigan Central Railway coming forward to meet his assistants. The man radiated power and dignity. Young Van Horne gazed at him with awe. He wondered if he might himself someday reach the same rank and travel about in a private car of his own.

"The glories of it, the pride of it, the salary … all that moved me deeply and I made up my mind then and there that I would reach it," he said. And he did. Just ten years later at the age of twenty-eight, he became the youngest railway superintendent in the world. Nobody in Canada had Van Horne's experience or expertise. After all, Canada had never built a railway as ambitious as the CPR.

His boss in the CPR was George Stephen, who was a financier, not a railroadman. A Scot, born in poverty, trained as a haberdasher, of all things, he had risen to be the president of the Bank of Montreal. Stephen was a Highlander. Van Horne was a mixture of Dutch, French and German. He had a quality of enthusiasm that Stephen must have admired, for Stephen had it too. When Stephen threw himself into a project, he went all the way. So did Van Horne. And what they were planning to do between them was to build the first transcontinental railway in Canadian history.

Stephen only had one passion – finance – unless you counted salmon fishing. But Van Horne had a half a dozen hobbies. He was a brilliant gardener and horticulturist; he even bred new varieties of plant life. He was an amateur geologist who had actually discovered and named new species of fossils; in fact, he carried a rock collection about with him. He was a clever cartoonist, a sketch artist, and an amateur magician.

Born in an Illinois log cabin, he had been left fatherless at eleven and at fourteen had to quit school to support his family. He was a hard worker but he played hard too. In his youth as a train dispatcher, his work day was twelve hours, but when it was over he didn't go home. Instead he hung around the yards and shops and offices, soaking up the railway business. He believed that any persistent person could always do what he set out to do.

One of Van Horne's first jobs was to fire General Thomas Rosser, who he felt was incompetent. As a result, the two almost got in a gun fight on the steps of the Manitoba Club in Winnipeg one hot July evening. Van Horne was no man to back away from a fight. As a child he had taken on every boy in school. The two men drew pistols, but others stepped in to prevent a shoot-out.

With Rosser out of the way in mid-February, 1882, Van Horne told Secretan, his replacement, that he wanted the "shortest commercial line" between Winnipeg and the Pacific coast. He said he would not only lay five hundred miles of track that summer, but would also have trains running over it by fall.

Secretan, a great, bulky Englishman with a waxed moustache, thought that was doubtful. Van Horne told him that nothing was impossible. If Secretan couldn't lay out the railroad, he said, then he would have his scalp. Van Horne didn't much like surveyors, but Secretan admired him as "the most versatile man I have encountered."

He noticed that as Van Horne talked he had a habit of making sketches on blotting pads, so well drawn that they were worth framing. Throughout his life, Van Horne had been a frustrated artist. As a small boy unable to afford paper, he had covered the whitewashed walls of his house with drawings. As a child he had fallen in love with a book called *Elementary Geology* – he liked it so much he decided to copy it. Night after night by candlelight the determined boy copied the book in ink onto sheets of foolscap – every page, every note, and every picture, right down to the index.

As he later admitted: "It taught me how much could be accomplished by application; it improved my handwriting; it taught me the construction of English sentences; and helped my drawing materially. And I never had to refer to the book again."

In later life he became a skilled amateur painter, attacking great canvasses as he attacked the building of the railway – with huge brushes at top speed. He believed that work was best done when it was done as rapidly as possible.

His drawings were so realistic that they were sometimes mistaken for actual engravings by other artists. He once got a copy of *Harper's Weekly Magazine* before it reached his mother and with great care transformed a series of portraits of American authors into bandits. He did it so well the pictures didn't appear to have been altered. His mother actually complained to the editor about his apparent policy of insulting the images of great Americans. The issue became a collector's item.

He had the high spirits of a small boy. He left one school because he drew caricatures of the principal. He was a bit of a joker and it cost him his first job when he set up an electric plate that gave a mild shock to any man who stepped on it. His boss stepped on it and fired him. As one of his colleagues said after he died, "He possessed a splendid simplicity of grownup boyhood to the end."

Van Horne loved to eat. When he was travelling around on the railway he used to wire ahead for roast chicken dinners to be set up for two, and when he arrived he'd eat both of them himself. He believed the men who worked for him should eat well too. Secretan had prepared a list of the food he needed in the field when he was surveying the line, but the company's new chief purchasing officer cut their order in half. Secretan made sure Van Horne heard about that. The general manager was indignant. After all, he knew what it was like to be hungry. So now he called the chief purchasing officer into his office and tore into him.

"Are you the God-forsaken idiot who buys the provisions? If so, I'll just give you till six o'clock tonight to ship a car-load of the very best stuff you can find up to Secretan, the engineer at the front; and see here, you can come back at six o'clock and tell me you have shipped it, you understand, but if you have not, you need not come back at all, but just go back to wherever you came from."

All that summer small luxuries continued to arrive at Secretan's camp.

But Van Horne faced greater problems than food. Some of his staff were against him because he hired more Americans than Canadians. But the Americans had railway building experience. Indeed, this most nationalistic of all Canadian enterprises was to a very large extent managed and built by Americans. No major railroad line had been built in Canada since the days of the Grand Trunk almost thirty years before.

Van Horne hired people he knew he could depend upon. Many of the Americans that came to Canada to build the CPR stayed on and became dedicated Canadians. As someone had remarked, the building of the CPR would make a Canadian out of the German Kaiser. It certainly made Canadians out of Van Horne and many of his colleagues. As Van Horne once told a newspaperman, "I'd keep the American idea out of this country."

That spring, serious floods had thrown out his careful schedule. Construction was held back for nearly a month. But Van Horne was making his presence felt. An iron man who never knew a moment's sickness, he didn't seem to need any sleep. Years later he summed up the secret of his stamina: "I eat all I can; I drink all I can; I smoke all I can and I don't give a damn for anything."

"Why do you want to go to bed?" he once asked Secretan. "It's a waste of time; and besides, you don't know what's going on." He could sit up all night in a poker game and then at seven o'clock rub his eyes, head for the office, and do a full day's work.

He was a great poker player. Indeed, he loved all card games. That may have been his secret – the ability to turn from one form of activity to another, to switch on and off, and not to get too anxious about any of his enterprises.

When Van Horne had finished his work he was free to play games, to eat a good supper, to smoke one of his gigantic cigars, to work with his rock specimens, or to beat a colleague at billiards or chess.

He loved to play and he loved to win. He didn't like to leave a poker table when he was losing. His memory for obscure detail was remarkable. He liked to dare his friends to duplicate the feats of memory with which he astonished everybody.

He was the terror of the railway, a kind of superman with an uncanny habit of always turning up just when things went wrong. Here's how one newspaper columnist in Winnipeg described the arrival of Van Horne at the unsuspecting settlement of Flat Creek west of Brandon.

"The trains run in a kind of go-as-you please style that is anything but refreshing to the general manager. But when Manager Van Horne strikes the town there is a shaking up of old bones. He cometh in like a blizzard and he goeth out like a lantern. He is the terror of Flat Krick. He shakes them up like an earthquake and they are as frightened of him as he were the old Nick himself. Yet Van Horne is calm and harmless looking. So is a she mule, and so is a buzz saw. You don't know their true inwardness till you go up and feel of them. To see Van Horne get out of the car and go softly up the platform, you would think he was an evangelist on his way west to preach temperance to the Mounted Police. But you are soon undeceived. If you are within hearing distance you will have more fun than you ever had in your life before. He cuffs the first official he comes to just to get his hand in and leads the next one out by the ear, and pointing eastward informs him the walking is good as far as St. Paul. To see the rest hunt their holes and commence scribbling for dear life is a terror. Van Horne wants to know. He is that kind of man. He wants to know why this was not done and why this was done. If the answers are not satisfactory there is a dark and bloody tragedy enacted right there. During each act all the characters are killed off and in the last scene the heavy villain is filled with dynamite, struck with a hammer, and by the time he has knocked a hole plumb through the sky, and the smoke has cleared away, Van Horne has discharged all the officials and hired them over again at lower figures."

As another railway president once remarked, "Van Horne was one of the most considerate and even-tempered of men, but when an explosion came it was magnificent."

Yet he rather enjoyed people who stood up to him. One was Michael J. Haney, a flamboyant Irish construction boss who was as tough as nails. Haney was in the Winnipeg freight yards one day when his secretary came hustling down the track to warn him that Van Horne was on the warpath.

"He's hot enough to melt rails," Haney was told. "If you've got any friends or relatives at home who are fond of you I'd advise you to hunt a cyclone cellar."

But Haney was feeling pretty hot himself. It was a

day on which everything had seemed to go wrong. And he was in a mood to look for somebody with trouble. So instead of getting out of Van Horne's way he stalked right down the yards to meet him.

Van Horne began an exhaustive lecture on the system's defects. His profanity turned the air blue. Haney waited until the general manager stopped for a breath, then lit into him.

"Mr. Van Horne," he said finally, "everything you say is true and if you claimed it was twice as bad as you have, it would still be true. I'm ready to agree with you there but I'd like to say this: Of all the spavined, one-horse, rottenly equipped, bad managed, badly run, headless and heedless thing for people to call a railroad, this is the worst. You can't get anyone who knows anything about anything. You can't get materials and if you could it wouldn't do you any good because you couldn't get them where you wanted them."

Haney followed up this outburst with a list of counter-complaints far longer than Van Horne's, since he was in closer touch with the work. His tirade made Van Horne's explosion "sound like a drawing room conversation." The general manager waited patiently as Haney unleashed his torrent of complaints; by the time Haney had finished he was grinning.

"That's all right, Haney. I guess we understand one another," he said. "Let's get to work."

CHAPTER THREE

Five hundred miles of steel

THE CONTRACT TO BUILD THE prairie section of the Canadian Pacific Railway was probably the largest of its kind ever undertaken. At the end of January, 1882, an American firm got the prize. There were two partners – General R.B. Langdon, a one-time stonemason of Scottish heritage, and D.C. Shepard, a former railroad engineer who had helped build the Chicago, Milwaukee and St. Paul Railroad.

The two men agreed to build 675 miles (1,080 km) of railroad across the plains from the end of track at Flat Creek in Manitoba to Fort Calgary on the Bow River in what is now Alberta. That was a formidable task. This section of the railway would only be fifteen miles (24 km) shorter than the entire length of the Central Pacific Railway in the U.S., which ran from California to Utah.

The day after the contract was signed, Langdon and Shepard advertised for three thousand men and four thousand horses. The work would have to be parcelled out to no fewer than three hundred sub-contractors hired to do specific jobs on specific sections of the line.

Between Flat Creek and Fort Calgary they would have to move ten million cubic yards (9.1 million cu. m) of earth. They'd have to haul every stick of timber, every rail, fish-plate, and spike, all the pilings used for bridge work, and all the food and provisions for 7,600 men and 1,700 teams of horses across the naked prairie for hundreds of miles.

To feed the horses alone they would have to distribute four thousand bushels (145,600 L) of oats every day along 150 miles (240 km) of track. No wonder his colleagues and rivals had laughed at Van Horne when he said he could build five hundred miles of that section in the one summer!

By the spring of 1882 Winnipeg was a gigantic supply depot. Stone began to pour in from every available quarry. Railroad ties came from Lake of the Woods country to the east, lumber from Minnesota, and rails from England and from the Krupp works in Germany.

Since the St. Lawrence would still be frozen well into the construction season, Van Horne had the steel shipped to New York and New Orleans, and transported to Manitoba by way of St. Paul along the St. Paul and Pacific Railway which ran between the American cities and Winnipeg.

Trainloads of material heading for the Canadian west were constantly passing through American cities. There, hundreds of checkers reported on them daily so that the exact moment of their arrival could be plotted.

As fast as the supplies arrived they were hauled to the "End of Track." Long trains loaded with rails, ties, fish-plates, and provisions rattled westward to Flat Creek, dumped their loads, and returned empty. No newly completed line of steel had ever known such activity in the first year of its construction.

Spring floods put a halt to all this activity, causing logjams of supplies in Winnipeg and St. Paul. The Red River valley was overflowing. The country between Winnipeg and Portage la Prairie looked like the ocean.

The Assiniboine near Brandon spilled over its banks and covered the valley. If the CPR bridge hadn't been held down by flat cars loaded with steel rails it would have been swept away. Settlers moving west had to move on foot and swim their cattle and horses across swollen rivers. Even oxen were sunk in the mud.

On the cart trail leading towards Qu'Appelle, a carpenter named William Oliver came across a strange spectacle of three wagons and six oxen, all lying half-buried in an ocean of gumbo. Their owners, six mud-caked Englishmen, sat helplessly by, downing a breakfast of bread and ale. Oliver hauled them out with the help of 200 feet (60 m) of rope.

The work came to a standstill. Flat Creek, which seemed to have more railway material piled up in its yards than any other place in the world, was a quagmire. Tents of every size and shape, some brand new and some filthy and tattered, stretched out in all directions on a gloomy expanse of swamp.

It was an entirely male population – freighters, farm labourers, bull-whackers, railroad navvies, muleteers, railway officials, and, of course, whiskey peddlers. There was no place to sleep. The food was terrible and sometimes non-existent. But Flat Creek's life was very brief. When the railroad blockade ended and the tracks began to creep west once more towards the newer community of Broadview, the town disappeared. Even the name was changed to the pleasanter one of Oak Lake.

By the time the floods ended, scores of would-be homesteaders were ready to quit the Northwest. Building was at a standstill in Brandon because the CPR was rushing all available construction materials to the front. Even before the floods began hundreds of men were idle.

The railway yards themselves looked like a great country fair. Trunks were piled up along the tracks like cordwood as high as men could throw them, but many of the owners were already trying to sell their outfits and leave.

In May a blizzard struck, destroying scores of tents and causing great suffering. Fuel was so scarce that men resorted to stealing lumber, stick by stick. One man, Charles Alfred Peyton, who lived in a small tent on the river bank at Brandon, would remember all his life trying to crawl on his stomach towards a pile of dry poles his neighbour had collected. Just as he seized a stick, a bullet whizzed through the wood not more than a foot away.

That was not uncommon. People began to tell each other it would be better to leave the land to the Indians. "Why should we take such a country away from them?" was heard on all sides. The first passenger train out of Brandon for the east after the flood contained three coaches loaded to the doors with men and women quitting the Northwest, never to return.

At last the water subsided, the blizzards ended, and the sun came out and warmed the frigid plains. The prairie evenings grew mellower. The sweet smell of wolf willow drifted in from the ponds and sloughs to mingle with the more familiar odours of salt pork, tamarack ties, wood smoke, and human sweat. The early spring blossoms – wild pansies, strawberries, and purple pasque flower – began to poke their tiny faces between the brittle grasses. Then as a flush of new green spread over the land, the oxcarts of the first settlers started west again until they were strung out by the hundreds ahead of the advancing line of steel.

Now a mountain of supplies descended upon Winnipeg. On a single day, May 15, eighteen thousand dollars' worth of freight poured into the city. The following day eighty freight cars arrived from St. Paul. The next day fifty thousand bushels (1,820,000 L) of oats and eleven carloads of mules were checked into the yards.

With the freight came people. By June three thousand immigrants were under canvas in Winnipeg, all buoyed up by the expectation of an entirely new life on the Canadian prairies. Few people now believed it would be possible for the CPR to achieve its season's goal or anything close to it after the delays.

But Van Horne was immovable. Langdon and Shepard had signed the contract promising to drive five hundred miles of steel that year. Five hundred miles it would have to

A trainload of stubborn pack mules arrives in Winnipeg in 1882.

be. The general manager made it clear he'd cancel the contract if they didn't live up to it.

And so they responded by increasing their army of men and horses. They added an extra shift to track-laying. They lengthened the total work day from eleven hours to fifteen. "The iron now is going down just as fast as it can be pulled from the cars," Shepard announced. "We shall show a record of track-laying which has never been surpassed on this continent."

A whirlwind of construction followed. One magazine called it "absolutely unparalleled in railway annals." The track, winding snakelike across the plains, moved so swiftly that Secretan and his surveyors were barely able to stay ahead. Sometimes, indeed, they were awakened at night by the rumble of giant scrapers being dragged past their tents. "We had never seen the like in Canada before," Secretan wrote in his memoirs.

CHAPTER FOUR

End of Track

THE PRAIRIE SECTION OF THE CPR was built like a telescope, extending from a single base. That, said a leading London journal, was impossible. But with Van Horne nothing was impossible. Winnipeg was the anchor point. From there the steel would stretch out for a thousand miles (1,600 km) into the mountains. There were no service roads, and no supply line for the railway builders other than the rails themselves.

The previous year's operations had seen small knots of men working in twos and threes with loaded handcars pushing the track forward at about three-quarters of a mile (1.2 km) a day. Van Horne aimed to move at five times that speed. That would require the kind of timing that army generals insist on in the field. Van Horne's army worked that summer with a military precision that astonished all who witnessed it. "Clockwork" was the term used over and over again.

The heart of the operation was at "End of Track" – a unique, mobile community that never stayed in one place for more than a few hours at a time. Here was a hive of industry in which teamsters, track-layers, blacksmiths, carpenters, executive officers, and other trades and professions all had a part. At the end of each day's work, this town on wheels moved another three or four miles (4.8 - 6.4 km) west.

The nerve centre of End of Track was the line of boarding cars – eight or nine of these, each three storeys high – that housed the track-laying crews. The ground floors served as offices, dining rooms, kitchens, and berths for contractors and company officials. The two storeys above were dormitories. Sometimes there were even tents pitched on the roofs.

These huge cars formed part of a long train which contained smaller office cars for executives, cooking cars, freight cars loaded with track materials, shops on wheels, and, on occasion, the private car of the general manager himself.

Van Horne was continually seen at End of Track, spinning yarns with workmen, sketching buffalo skulls, organizing foot races and target shooting at night, and bumping over the prairie in a buckboard inspecting the track.

Every day some sixty-five carloads of railroad supplies, each carload weighing eighteen tons (16 tonnes), were dumped at End of Track. Most of these supplies had been carried an average of a thousand miles (1,600 km) before reaching their destination.

To a casual visitor this scene was chaotic: cars constantly

being coupled and uncoupled, locomotives shunting back and forth, pushing and pulling loads of various lengths, little handcars rattling up and down the half-completed track at the front, teams of horses and mules dragging loaded wagons forward on each side of the main line – and tents constantly rising like puffballs and vanishing again as the whole apparatus rolled steadily towards the Rocky Mountains.

Actually this confusion was an illusion. The organization was carefully planned, down to the last railway spike.

End of Track – the nerve centre of railroad-building operations.

Each morning two construction trains set out from the supply yards far in the rear, heading for End of Track. Each train was loaded with the exact number of rails, ties, spikes, fishplates, and telegraph poles required for half a mile (800 m) of railway. One train was held in reserve on a siding about six miles (9.6 km) to the rear, while the other moved directly to the front, where the track-laying gang of three hundred men and seventy horses waited for it.

The track-layers worked like a drill team. "It was beautiful to watch them gradually coming near," one observer

wrote, "each man in his place knowing exactly his work and doing it at the right time and in the right way. Onward they come, pass on, and leave the wondering spectator slowly behind while he is still engrossed with the wonderful sight." The ties were unloaded first on either side of the track. They were to be picked up by the waiting wagons and mule teams – thirty ties to a wagon – and hauled forward and dropped along the embankment for exactly half a mile. Two men with marked rods were standing by. As the ties were thrown out, they laid them across the grade, exactly two feet (0.6 m) apart from centre to centre.

Right behind the teams came a hand truck hauled by two horses, one on each side of the track, each loaded with rails, spikes, and fishplates, which held the ties down. Six men marched on each side of the track, and when they reached the far end of the last pair of newly-laid rails, each crew seized a rail among them and threw it into the exact position. Two men gauged these rails to make sure they were correctly aligned. Four men followed with spikes, placing one on each end of the four ends of the rails, four others screwed in the fishplates, and another four followed with crowbars to raise the ties while the spikes were being hammered in.

All these men worked in a kind of a rhythm, each man directly opposite his partner on each separate rail. More men followed with hammers and spikes to make the rail secure. By this time the hand truck had already moved forward over the newly-laid rails even before the job was finished. All the men had to keep in their places and move on ahead, otherwise they would be caught up by those behind them.

As each construction train dumped its half-mile of supplies at End of Track, it moved back to the nearest siding to be replaced by the reserve train. No time was lost. As the track unfolded, the boarding cars were nudged ahead constantly by the construction train locomotive so that no energy would be wasted by the navvies in reaching their moving mess halls and dormitories.

The operation was strung out for hundreds of miles across the open prairie. Far in advance were the survey camps. These were followed by the grading gangs, scraping the soil off the prairie. Behind them came the bridge-builders. Far to the rear were other thousands – saddlers and carpenters, cooks and tailors, shoemakers, blacksmiths, doctors and provisioners.

Vast material yards were set up at hundred-mile (160 km) intervals between Winnipeg and End of Track. Supply trains moved out on schedule heading west, unloading thousands of tons of goods at the yards. There all the material was sorted daily into train lots and sent off – as many as eight trains a day – to the front.

Nothing was left to chance. Just in case the track-laying should move faster than expected, extra supplies were held on the sidings and in the yards themselves. Thus, there were enough rails always available for three hundred miles (480 km) and enough fastenings for five hundred (800 km), all within a hundred miles of End of Track.

When the steel moved past the hundred-mile point, the

SURVEYORS

FISHPLATE

SPIKE

GRADING

The building of the CPR.

yards moved too. An entire community of office workers, sorters, dispatchers, trainmen, labourers, and often their families as well, could be moved a hundred miles in a single night without the loss of an hour's work. The houses were portable and easily fitted onto the flat cars.

The telegraph teams moved right behind the track-layers. They camped in tents, moving their gear forward every afternoon on handcars. The construction trains that brought half a mile (0.8 km) of track supplies also brought half a mile of poles, wires, and insulators for the front. And so, just one hour after the day's track was laid, End of Track was in telegraphic communication with the outside world.

Miles to the west on the barren plain the bridging crews, grading units, and survey teams felt themselves driven forward by the knowledge that the track-layers were pressing hard behind. The work was so arranged that no weak link could hold up construction. The head contractor had a special group standing by prepared to finish any work that seemed unlikely to be ready in time for the track to be laid.

The grading was done by immense scrapers pulled by teams of horses. It was their job to build an embankment for the railway four feet (1.2 m) above the prairie and to ditch it for twenty yards (18.3 m) on each side. At that height the rails would be protected from the blizzards of winter and costly delays from snow blockage could be avoided.

The bridgers worked in two gangs, one by day, one by night. Every sliver of bridging had to be brought from Rat

Portage (now Kenora), 140 miles (224 km) east of Winnipeg, or from Minnesota south of the border. Thus the bridge-builders were seldom more than ten miles (16 km) ahead of the advancing steel. The timbers were unloaded as close to End of Track as possible and mostly at night so as not to interfere with other work.

The nation was amazed at the speed with which the railway was being forced across the plains. One man said it seemed to move as fast as the oxcarts of the settlers who were following along behind.

The Northwest was being transformed by the onslaught of the rails. One young man and his sweetheart were able to elope successfully by commandeering a handcar and speeding towards Winnipeg along the line of steel, thus throwing off their pursuers.

The progress of construction was so swift that antelope and other game migrating north were cut off on their return that fall by the lines of rails and telephone posts. They gathered by the hundreds on the north side, afraid to cross it. This would be the last summer in which herds of buffalo and antelope would freely roam the prairie.

Father Albert Lacombe, the voyageur priest who had spent so many years ministering to the Indians of the Northwest, watched the approach of the rails with both sadness and resignation:

"I would look in silence at that road coming on – like a band of wild geese in the sky – cutting its way through the prairies; opening up the great country we thought would be ours for years. Like a vision I could see it driving my poor Indians before it, and spreading out behind it the farms, the towns and cities …. No one who has not lived in the west since the Old-Times can realize what is due to that road – that CPR. It was Magic – like the mirage on the prairies, changing the face of the whole country."

The Indians watched in silence as the steel cut through their hunting grounds. They would arrive suddenly, squat on their haunches in double rows, and take in the scene with only the occasional surprised murmur. If they realized their wild, free existence was at an end, they gave no sign.

Onward the track moved, cutting the prairies in two. It moved through a land of geese, snipe, and wild ducks, whose eggs the navvies searched out and ate. It moved through a country fragrant in the soft evenings with a scent of willow and balsam. It cut across fields of yellow daisies, tiger lilies, purple sage, and briar rose. It bisected pastures of waist-high buffalo grass and skirted green hay meadows which, in the spring, were shallow ponds.

As it travelled westward it pushed through a country of memories and old bones – furrowed trails made decades before by thousands of bison moving in single file towards the water – vast fields of grey and withered brush, dead lakes rimmed with tell-tale crusts of alkali.

Day by day it crept toward the horizon. There, against the gold of the sunset, flocks of fluttering wild fowl, disturbed by the clamour of the invaders, could be seen in silhouette. Sometimes a single Indian, galloping at full speed in the distance, became no more than a speck crawling along the rim of the prairie.

This had been once known as the Great Lone Land, unfenced and unbridged. The line of steel made that phrase out of date, for the land would never again be lonely. All that summer it rang with a clang of sledge and anvil, the snorting of horses and mules, the hoarse puffing of great engines, the bellowing of section bosses, the curses of sweating thousands.

History was being made, but few had time to note that fact. William Oliver, a carpenter and future mayor of Lethbridge moving west in his oxcart, had no time to think of history. Later he wrote: "It never came to my mind in watching the building of the railway ... that in the next fifty years it would play so important a part in the commerce of the country and in fact of the world.... We were more interested in our own affairs and the prospects of a future home...."

The railroad workmen – known as "navvies" – were a mixed lot. They ranged all the way from a gang of Italians who "looked like guys who would cut your throat for a dime," as one observer put it, to younger sons of wealthy Englishmen and graduates of public schools. Some came for adventure, some because they wanted to become Canadians, some because they were down on their luck, and some because the pay was good.

A Winnipeg newspaperman was introduced to a track-laying gang by a section boss who identified some of them:

"Do you see that person yonder, that man can read and write Greek and is one of the most profound scholars on the continent; that man next him was once one of the foremost surgeons in Montreal, and that man next to him was at one time the beloved pastor of one of the largest congregations in Chicago."

The navvies were paid between $2.00 and $2.50 a day – good wages for those times. Often, after they made a little money they quit. Swedes who had learned how to lay track in the old country were highly prized. One Broadview pioneer claimed that "if they were given enough liquor they could lay two or three miles of track in a day." But liquor was prohibited by law in the Northwest although it existed in private hiding places all along the line. The construction workers were plagued by whiskey peddlers who sold a mixture which was described as "a mixture of blue ruin, chain lightning, strychnine, the curse of God and old rye."

As autumn approached the pace quickened. At the end of August one crew managed to lay four and half miles (7.2 km) of steel in a single day. Next day they beat their own record and laid five miles (8 km).

It was all horribly expensive. There were those who thought that Van Horne "seemed to spend money like a whole navy of drunken sailors." Actually he counted every dollar. In the interests of both speed and economy he allowed steep grades and tight curves which he planned to eliminate once the line was operating.

The contractors didn't reach their goal of five hundred

miles – the spring floods had prevented that. However, by the end of the season they had laid 417 miles (667 km) of completed railroad, built twenty-eight miles (45 km) of sidings, and graded another eighteen miles (24 km) for the start of the next season. In addition, Van Horne had pushed the southwestern branch line of the CPR in Manitoba a hundred miles (160 km) and so he could say that, in one way or another, he had achieved what he sought.

The public thought that he had worked a miracle.

CHAPTER FIVE

The birth of Regina

WITH THE RAILS SPEEDING WEST AT top speed and the settlers moving behind them, it was necessary to establish a capital for the new North West Territories. This vast area included all the land between the Rocky Mountains and the province of Manitoba from the forty-ninth parallel to the Arctic.

The original capital had been Battleford on the North Saskatchewan River. But Battleford was no longer on the route of the railway and so it no longer counted. The new capital, wherever it was, would be the most important city between the Red River and the Bow, in the foothills of the Rockies. And, because the capital would have to be at a divisional point on the line, the owners of the railway would have a good deal to say about its selection.

The man picked by the prime minister, Sir John A. Macdonald, to choose the site of the new capital was the Honourable Edgar Dewdney. He was lieutenant-governor of the North West Territories and Indian commissioner as well. A handsome giant, with his fringed buckskin jacket

Edgar Dewdney, lieutenant-governor of the North West Territories, picks Regina as the new territorial capital.

and his flaring mutton-chop whiskers, he made an imposing figure as he stalked about accompanied by his huge Newfoundland dogs.

The speculators knew that when the site was chosen it would become the most profitable piece of real estate in the country. Throughout the winter of 1881-82 they had been sending bands of men to occupy every prominent location. That is one reason why the CPR changed its survey in Saskatchewan and moved the line about six miles (9.6 km) to the south. The company wanted to frustrate the profit takers.

One likely townsite had been at the crossing of the Wascana or Pile o' Bones Creek. Wascana is a corruption of a Cree word "Oskana" meaning "bones." The bleached skeletons of thousands of buffalo lay in heaps along the banks of the river – hence the name – marking the site of an old buffalo corral into which the Indians had driven the bison to be slaughtered.

Because water was so scarce, the riverbank seemed a probable site, not only to the first surveyors, but also to the squatters who followed and sometimes got ahead of them. Not far from the pile of buffalo bones was a well-wooded area, where the original survey line crossed the creek. But when the railway was moved a half dozen miles to the south the land sharks were left out in the cold.

That change in the route took place on May 13, 1882. At the time there were only three settlers on the dry and treeless plain at the point where the new line crossed the creek. One of these was a surveyor himself, Thomas Gore.

The new site, Gore said, was "by far the best I've seen in the North West."

Most of the speculators and settlers disagreed. They felt that the only possible site for a capital city of the plains lay a few miles to the northeast in the broad, wooded valley of the Qu'Appelle River, one of the loveliest spots on the prairies.

Everything that was needed for a townsite was there – an established community, plenty of sweet water, sheltering hills, good drainage, and timber for fuel, lumber, and shade.

The railway builders, however, planned to skirt Qu'Appelle. They claimed the banks of the valley were too steep. Probably more important was the company's policy of bypassing settled communities in the interests of greater land profits. There were just too many squatters looking for easy money in the Qu'Appelle area.

Another factor was Governor Dewdney's own interest in the land surrounding Pile o' Bones crossing. He and several friends had formed two syndicates in great secrecy to purchase big chunks of Hudson's Bay Company land along the future route of the railway. One of these syndicates owned 480 acres (194 hectares) on the very spot that Dewdney now selected as a site of the future capital.

The property, of course, was not bought in Dewdney's name, but in the name of a trustee. All the other members of the syndicate kept their names secret; they stood to profit greatly if their land was chosen for the capital.

Dewdney himself was a surveyor. He had helped to lay

out the town of New Westminster, and also the trails and roads between the communities that led to the Cariboo gold fields in the B.C. interior. He was also a close supporter of the prime minister and was now prepared to reap the rewards of that support. And so there he was, suffering from rheumatism, hobbling about on a stick that May, as he examined the banks of Pile o' Bones Creek.

A few days later a man named William White arrived – he had learned that the line had been moved and so he and five others made a dash for the new townsite. They brought a complete farming outfit, a yoke of oxen, tents, wagons, bobsleighs, and provisions. They took the train as far as Brandon and in mid-April pushed off into the snows, which were then two feet (0.6 m) deep on the trails.

The ruts on the trail were so deep and the ponds so treacherous the party rarely covered more than a dozen miles (19 km) a day. In fact, on one day it took them seven hours to move two miles (3.2 km). When they reached Pile o' Bones Creek they almost drowned when the ferry sank in midstream from overloading. On May 17 they were caught by a shrieking blizzard that held them for three nights; but on May 20 they reached their goal.

White immediately grabbed a 160-acre (65 hectares) homestead near the banks of the river where the survey line crossed it. This was to be the exact site of the business section of the new capital. To White it looked so desolate he couldn't believe anyone would be foolish enough to locate a capital city on that naked plain. He gave up his homestead and took another two miles (3.2 km) away, thereby losing one of the most valuable parcels of real estate on the prairies.

By this time rumours were flying in the Qu'Appelle valley about the choice of a new capital. More tents were rising. Speculators were keeping a careful watch on Dewdney. In the midst of the Dominion Day festivities Dewdney took advantage of the celebration to slip quietly away. Late in the afternoon of June 30 he posted a notice near Thomas Gore's tent, reserving for the government all the land in the vicinity. His own syndicate property adjoined the government reserve directly to the north.

And so the city of Regina, as yet unnamed, was quietly established. When the news reached Fort Qu'Appelle there was frustration, disappointment, and frenzy. Most of the settlers hitched up their teams and moved everything to the banks of Pile o' Bones Creek. Squatters, advancing like an army, poured towards the embryo city. A few were bona fide homesteaders. Most were Winnipeg speculators, or people who had been paid by these speculators to squat on the land and hold it.

By mid-August the word was out: the capital would be on Pile o' Bones Creek. It was not announced officially until the following March. The governor-general, Lord Lorne, was consulted about the name. He left the matter to his wife, Princess Louise, and she chose Regina in honour of her mother, Queen Victoria.

Nobody liked that name. Princess Louise was not very

popular. Her boredom with Ottawa was widely known. The *Winnipeg Sun* ran a poll of leading citizens on the subject of the name. "That's a fool of a name," cried Joseph Wolf, a well known auctioneer who wanted an Indian name. Another citizen, Fred Scoble, referred to the name as "a double-barrelled forty-horse-power fool of a name." A third insisted on calling the city "Re-join-her."

The choice of the site caused even more controversy than the name. When the Canadian Press Association visited the townsite in August, the eastern reporters were dismayed to find nothing more than a cluster of tattered tents huddled together on a bald and arid plain. One paper called it a "huge swindle." Another said it should have been named "Golgotha" because of its barren setting.

As the Toronto *World* declared, "No one has a good word for Regina." To Peter McAra, who later became its mayor, Regina was "just about as unlovely a site as one could well imagine." Even George Stephen, the president of the CPR, was dubious. He would have preferred Moose Jaw.

But Dewdney believed he had chosen the best possible location. He had told Macdonald (quite accurately, as it turned out) that the new capital was in the very heart of the best wheat district in the country. That statement was greeted with jeers because it was well known that he and his partners stood to make a million and a half dollars from their property if they could sell it.

Dewdney's Regina interests inevitably led to a clash with the CPR. The railway was already hard-pressed for funds. Its main asset was the land it owned on the sites of new towns. It didn't intend to share these real estate profits with outsiders.

Its interests were identical with those of the government, which was also in the land business in Regina. Under the terms of the CPR contract, the railway owned odd-numbered sections along the railway right of way, except for those originally granted to the Hudson's Bay Company. In Regina and in several other important prairie towns, the government and the CPR pooled their land interests, placed them under joint management, and shared the profits.

That summer, the railway, in order to raise funds, agreed to sell an immense slice of its land – five million acres (2,023,500 hectares) – to a British-Canadian syndicate, the Canada North-West Land Company. The company would manage land sales in forty-seven major communities, including Moose Jaw, Calgary, Regina, Swift Current, and Medicine Hat. The railway would get half the net profits. And so in Regina a quarter of the land profits went to the railway, a quarter to the land company, and one half to the government.

Now there was a struggle between Dewdney on one side and the land company and the railway on the other, as to where the public buildings of Regina were to be situated. The railway, of course, wanted the centre of the new capital on its own lands and those owned by the government. Edgar Dewdney wanted them on his property.

The CPR had the advantage. It could locate the railway station anywhere it wanted and wherever the railway station was, the business section would follow. And so it built its station two miles (3.2 km) east of Dewdney's river property in a small and muddy depression far from any natural source of water.

As a result Regina began at first to grow up on two locations. The magnet of the station was too much for the settlers whose tents started to rise in clusters on the swampy triangle known as The Gore in front of the makeshift terminal.

Both sides attempted to sell land. Dewdney's syndicate tried to show that its land was the most popular and pointed out that the railway land lacked water. The railway countered by promising a large reservoir that would supply the city.

Of course, the railway won. It sold a half million dollars' worth of real estate that winter. The Dewdney syndicate sold very little.

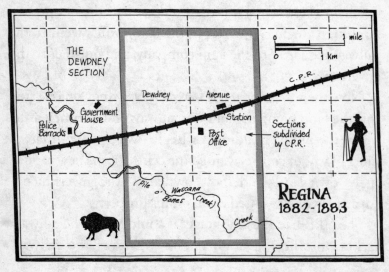

There was a second struggle: where to put the government buildings? Dewdney, naturally, wanted them near the river next door to his own land. The railway and the government wanted them near the station. In the end the police barracks and the lieutenant-governor's residence were on the river, but the customs office, the land office, and eventually the post office were placed near the station, two miles away. The offices of the Indian commissioner and North West Council were placed halfway between the station and the river. Later, when the registry office went up, it was on a block of its own.

And so the queer community straggled for two and a half miles (4 km) across the prairies, the various clusters of official buildings standing like islands in the prairie sea. Regina was a city without a centre.

CHAPTER SIX

The promised land

B Y THE SPRING OF 1883 CANADA WAS A country with half a transcontinental railroad. Track lay in pieces like a child's train set – long stretches of finished road separated by large gaps. But a continuous line of steel now ran 937 miles (1500 km) from Fort William at the head of Lake Superior to the tent community of Swift Current.

As the track began to move west again on the prairie section, thousands of people were invading the land of the Blackfoot. Little steel shoots were sprouting south, west, and east of the main trunk line in Manitoba. And wherever the steel went, the settlers followed with their tents and their tools, their cattle and their kittens, their furniture and their fences.

They poured in from the famine-ridden bog country of Ireland, the bleak crofts of the Scottish hills, and the smoky hives of industrial England. The land moved past them like a series of painted scenes on flash cards – a confused impression of station platforms and very little more, because the windows in the wooden cars were too high and too small to give much of a view of the new world.

They sat crowded together on hard seats that ran length-wise, and they cooked their own food at a wood stove placed in the centre of the car. They were patient people, full of hope, blessed by good cheer. In the spring and summer of 1883, some 133,000 arrived in Canada. Of that number, two-thirds sped directly to the Northwest.

No one had expected such an onslaught. The demand for passage across the Atlantic was unprecedented. The CPR didn't have enough trains to handle the invading army. It was forced to use its dwindling reserve of cash to buy additional colonist cars second-hand.

In Toronto, in May alone ten thousand meals were served in the overflowing immigrant sheds – as many as had been prepared in the entire season of 1882. The young Canadian postal service was flooded with twelve thousand letters destined for the Northwest. The number had quadrupled in just two years.

The settlers from the old world – some had come from places as remote as Iceland – had been joined by farmers from the back roads of Ontario. Off to the west the trains puffed, every car crammed with people clinging to the steps and all singing the song that became the pioneer theme, "One More River to Cross." By April the CPR was able to take them as far as the tent community of Moose Jaw, four hundred miles (640 km) west of Winnipeg, and sometimes 150 miles (240 km) further on to Swift Current.

As many as twenty-five hundred settlers left Winnipeg every week. It was impossible to tell blue blood from peasant. The man in the next homestead or the worker serving in the tent restaurant might be of noble birth.

The son of the English poet laureate Alfred, Lord Tennyson, was breaking sod on a homestead that spring. Nicholas Flood Davin, a well known journalist, on his first day in Regina was impressed by the manner of a waiter in the tent where he took breakfast. The waiter turned out to be the nephew of a duke. He was helping to manage a tent-hotel for the nephew of an earl.

Many settlers arrived without funds. They brought everything to the prairies from pet kittens to canaries. One arrived with a crate full of cats, which were snapped up at three dollars apiece by immigrants lonely for company of any kind. Another early pioneer, Esther Goldsmith, always remembered the wild scene at the Brandon station where a birdcage was sucked from a woman's hand in the scramble for the train. A typical menagerie was brought to Moosomin in 1883 by the Hislop family. It included two horses, four cows, three sheep, a little white sow, a dog, a cat, eleven hens, and a rooster.

It was gruelling work for settlers to break up the prairie sod. The land was dotted with small rose bushes whose interwoven roots added to the toughness of the turf. A man with a good team of oxen was lucky if he could till three-quarters of an acre (a third of a hectare) in a day. It was a harsher life than most had bargained for.

Most settlers counted themselves lucky that first year if they could build a hovel out of the hard-packed sod. One typical sod house built near Regina in the fall of 1884 consisted of a big cellar dug out of the side of a hill, over which were laid poles in the shape of a gabled roof, the ends resting on the ground. On top of these was placed hay to the depth of a foot and over the hay huge squares of sod chinked with dried earth. At the ends of the gables were small poles plastered together with a mortar of yellow clay and straw. Tiny windows were cut in one end and a door in the other. The floor was a mixture of clay and straw and water, about six inches (15 cm) thick, tamped tightly to the ground. The inside walls and ceiling were plastered with mud and then whitewashed. In such cave-like dwellings entire families existed winter after winter. The central piece of furniture and sole source of heat was the cookstove.

Few settlers saw the inside of a general store more than once or twice a year. For most, a shopping trip meant an exhausting journey fifty or a hundred miles (80 to 160 km) by oxcart. Pork was a staple meat, when meat was available at all. Molasses did duty for sugar. Coffee was often synthetic, made from roasted barley, rye, or wheat — or even toast crumbs.

Many a settler lived almost entirely on potatoes, bread, treacle, porridge and rabbit stew. Often families went hungry. John Wilson of Saltcoats always remembered the winter of 1883 when, as a boy of seven, he and other members of his family were reduced to a single slice of bread each three times a day. The snow was so deep they couldn't reach their nearest neighbours six miles (9.6 km) away.

Nine-year-old May Clark arrived in Regina from England with her family on a soaking wet day in May, 1883. They expected to find a town in the old country sense. Instead they discovered a ragged cluster of tents rising from the muddy prairie. When they were sent to a hotel they found it was a tent too, with nothing between their bedroom and the next but a partition of stretched blankets.

Regina that spring was mainly a city of women and children. Most of the men were off on the prairie looking for a homestead. After several days May's father located a suitable quarter-section about thirteen miles (21 km) to the northeast. The six members of the family packed everything, including pigs and chickens and bowie knife to ward off "wild Indians," and then took a covered wagon – or prairie schooner, as it was called – across the hummocky plain behind two oxen, with a milk cow bringing up the rear.

They seemed totally unfitted for pioneer life. May's mother was sickly and frail. Her father, thin-faced and pale, had never driven a team before. They were used to the gentle beauty of the English Midlands and were appalled by the sweeping loneliness of the prairie.

When the Clark family first reached their homestead it seemed as remote as a desert island. There was nothing to be seen to the distant horizon. There was a vague smudge off to the north which the children were told was a copse of trees. That was all.

The Clarks spent their first summer tilling a few acres of

soil and trying to build a log house. Septimus Clark over-strained himself and was confined to his bed. When he recovered he found he did not know how to build the roof, doors, or windows. There was never enough to eat. The children were always hungry. They tried to fill their stomachs with wild leaves and berries. Polly, the cow, refused to give milk. One night both parents became lost on the open prairie, and the children spent a terrifying twelve hours alone wondering if they would ever see them again.

In spite of it all, the family survived and thrived in both health and spirits. Hard work acted as a tonic. Life may have been harsh, but it was clearly invigorating. When May Clark, who became Mrs. Hartford Davis, published her memoirs at the age of eighty-one, four of the five Clark children were still alive to share them.

Government land such as the Clarks' was free up to a limit of a quarter-section – 160 acres (65 hectares). Anybody who worked it for three years could have it. And you could also take on the next quarter-section. If you bought CPR land along the railway you paid five dollars an acre but got back $3.75 if you were able to crop three-quarters of it within four years.

Meanwhile, as the rails pushed steadily towards the mountains, new communities began to take shape. "These towns along the line west of Brandon are all the same. See one, see all," the Fort MacLeod *Gazette* reported. They all had the same houses, mostly board frames with a canvas roof. Moose Jaw with its "bare, freckled and sunburnt buildings" and Medicine Hat, another canvas town, were in this category. And yet Moose Jaw already had three newspapers and six hotels, though most of these were mere tents.

And still the trains roared by to End of Track. By July of 1883 the organization had been perfected to the point where ninety-seven miles (155 km) of track were laid instead of the monthly average of fifty-eight (93 km).

As Langdon and Shepard approached the end of their contract, the track-laying guides were seized by a kind of frenzy. On July 28, about two weeks out of Calgary, they set another record. It's one that has never been surpassed for manual labour on a railroad: 6.38 miles (10.2 km) of finished railway — earthworks, grading, track-laying and ballasting — were completed in a single day.

It was, of course, a stunt. Special men were brought in, including the tireless Ryan brothers, world champion spikers, who could drive a spike home with two blows, and Big Jack, a Herculean Swede who was said to be able to hoist a thirty-foot (9 m) rail weighing 560 pounds (254 kg) and heave it onto a flat car without assistance.

The city of Calgary was not yet born, but some of its future citizens were at work along the line of track oblivious to the fact they would help to build the foothills community. Turner Bone, a railway engineer, recalled in his memoirs how many of the men he bumped into later became prominent Calgarians. When Bone arrived in Moose Jaw late one night, the CPR's watchman guided him with the aid of a sputtering lantern to a large marquee pretentiously named

Royal Hotel. This man was Thomas Burns – he later became a city assessor and city treasurer of Calgary. In a Medicine Hat office he encountered a messenger boy just twelve years old, who answered to the name of George. He became the mayor of Calgary, George Webster.

In the company boarding house Bone ran into a former supply officer who had opened a law office in Medicine Hat. This was James Lougheed, soon to become the most noted lawyer in the West, Conservative leader in the Senate, cabinet minister in the Canadian government, and the grandfather of a future premier of Alberta, Peter Lougheed.

As the railway towns began to prosper, jealousies sprang up between nearby communities. A three-cornered battle took place between Winnipeg, Moose Jaw, and Regina. The argument, supposedly over the choice of Regina as the capital, was really over real estate.

The battle was fought out in the newspapers. But Regina had none and so a group of citizens got together, raised $5,000, and talked Nicholas Flood Davin, one of the most distinguished journalists in Canada, to start the Regina *Leader*.

Davin named it that because he intended to make it the leading newspaper in the northwest, and in this he was successful. Once established, he struck back at Regina's critics. He referred to Moose Jaw as "Loose Jaw" and engaged in a running battle with that town's newspaper. He attacked the real estate sharks trying to get the capital moved and, when he ran out of prose, he turned to poetry.

Five thousand dollars was a lot of money for Regina to raise in the 1880s – it was enough to keep a man and his family in luxury for four years. But reading Nicholas Flood Davin's sweet invective, the citizens who paid the editor's bonus must have reckoned that they had been given their money's worth.

CHAPTER SEVEN

~
The displaced people

THE WHOLE COUNTRY MARVELLED THAT spring and summer of 1883 over the feat of building the railway across the prairies – everybody except the people it was displacing.

To the Indians the railway symbolized the end of a golden age. The natives, liberated by the white man's horses and the white man's weapons, had galloped freely across the open prairie for more than a hundred years. The game seemed unlimited, and the zest of the hunt gave life a tang and a purpose. This charmed existence came to an end with the suddenness of a thunderclap, just as the railway, like a glittering spear, was thrust through the ancient hunting grounds of the Blackfoot and Cree.

Within six years the image of the Plains Indian underwent a total transformation. From proud and fearless nomads, rich in culture and tradition, they became pathetic, half-starved creatures, confined to the semi-prisons of their new reserves, and totally dependent on government relief for their existence. Actually, the buffalo on which the Indian depended were gone before the railway came, victims of the white man's overkill. But they could not have survived on a land bisected by steel and criss-crossed by barbed wire.

Without the buffalo, which had supplied them with food, shelter, clothing, tools, and ornaments, the Indians were helpless. By 1880, after the three most terrible years they had ever known, they were forced to eat their dogs and their horses, to scrabble for gophers and mice, and even to consume the carcasses of animals they found rotting on the prairie.

On top of this they were faced with a totally foreign culture. And the railway made that impact immediate. It did not arrive gradually as it had in eastern Canada. In the Northwest it happened in the space of a few years.

The government's policy was a two-stage one. The starving Indians would be fed at public expense – temporarily. Over a longer period, the Indian Department would try to bring about a change that usually took centuries. It would try to turn a race of hunters into a community of peasants. The Indians, in short, would become farmers – or that was the idea. The Indian reserves would be on land north of the railway, far from the hunting grounds, and so the CPR became the visible symbol of the Indians' tragedy.

The famine had been so great that thousands of Indians reluctantly trekked to the new reserves. Others, led by such Cree chieftains as Big Bear and Piapot, continued to oppose the authorities, hoping to hunt the non-existent buffalo. By the winter of 1882-83, with the railway snaking across the prairies, five thousand disillusioned Indians were starving in the neighbourhood of Fort Walsh south of Calgary. In the end everybody moved north to the reserves. To the south lay the railway – a steel fence barring them from their past.

The native peoples, Cree and Blackfoot, had no concept of the white man's idea of "real estate." In their society, land was not something that was *owned*, any more than the air or the waters were owned. The whole principle of private property was foreign to them. The idea of fencing in the prairie, parcelling it out to strangers, buying it and selling it for profit, was difficult to grasp. For white Canadians, the coming of the railway was the climax of a grand plan for a nation extending from sea to sea. For the native peoples it was a cultural disaster, the tragic consequences of which have lasted until our time.

Some of the chiefs accepted the coming of steel fatalistically. Chief Poundmaker, for instance, urged his followers to prepare for it. He had negotiated a treaty with the Canadian government in 1879 and settled on the reserve on the Battle River. But when he realized the buffalo were gone he told his people to work hard, plant grain, and take care of their cattle.

On the other hand, Chief Piapot ran afoul of survey crews in 1882 and pulled up forty miles (64 km) of surveyors' stakes west of Moose Jaw. These were his hunting grounds, and he ordered his people to camp directly upon the right of way. He blamed the railway for all his troubles.

Many of the native peoples greeted the stories of the

snorting locomotives with disbelief. They watched the construction in silence. The women pulled their shawls over their heads in terror of the whistle, and refused to cross streams on the new trestles, preferring to wade up to their armpits. Some of the younger men, their faces painted brilliant scarlet, would try to race the train on their swift ponies. Few would actually touch the cars.

Piapot believed the smoke of the locomotives was evil medicine that would ruin his people. His fears were not groundless, but his personal appeal to the lieutenant-governor was fruitless.

Young natives race a CPR train on their horses.

Not far from Calgary the railway builders encountered the most remarkable Indian leader of all – Crowfoot, chief of the Blackfoot nation. A slender, intelligent man with a classic Roman nose, he carried himself with great dignity and was renowned for many feats of bravery. He had fought in nineteen battles, been wounded six times, and had once rescued a child from the jaws of a grizzly bear, killing the animal with a spear while the whole camp watched.

He had many good qualities – eloquence, political skill, charity, and, above all, foresight. Long before his people he foresaw the end of the buffalo, and so signed a treaty in

1877. When the tents of the construction workers went up on the borders of his reserve there was anger and bitterness among the tribe. The white man was invading the land of the Blackfoot. The chief sent messengers to warn a foreman that no further construction work would be allowed. Seven hundred armed braves stood ready to attack.

At this point, Father Albert Lacombe, the Oblate missionary to the Blackfoot band, stepped into the picture. He, too, had been concerned about the creeping advance of civilization. When he learned of the trouble on the reserve, he rode immediately to the construction camp – a homely priest in a tattered cassock, bumping over the prairie, his silver curls streaming out from beneath his black hat.

At End of Track Lacombe met with a rude rejection. He was told the Indians could go to the devil. And so he made his appeal to a higher authority. Lacombe knew Van Horne, having met him during his term as chaplain to the railway workers in the Thunder Bay branch. Now he sent him a telegram. Back came the order straight to End of Track – cease all work until the Indians are satisfied. Lacombe was asked to appease the Blackfoot any way he could.

The priest had known Crowfoot for years. Once he had led a party of starving Crees for twenty-two days through a blizzard to apparently miraculous safety. Another time, when an entire Blackfoot camp came down with scarlet fever, he had worked tirelessly for twenty days among the sick before he himself contracted the disease. When he nursed the Indians during a smallpox epidemic in 1870,

Father Albert Lacombe speaks to Chief Crowfoot and his Blackfoot tribe about the coming of the railroad.

hundreds were so moved by his selflessness that they became Christians.

Now the priest set out to placate his old friend. He came into the camp bearing gifts: two hundred pounds (91 kg) of sugar and a similar amount of tobacco, tea, and flour. Then Crowfoot called a grand council where the priest, standing before the squatting braves, spoke.

"Now my mouth is open; you people listen to my words. If one of you can say that for the fifteen years I have lived among you, I have given you bad advice, let him rise and speak...."

No one budged. It was a dangerous, electric situation. Lacombe kept on:

"Well, my friends, I have some advice to give you today. Let the white people pass through your lands and let them build their roads. They are not here to rob you of your lands. These white men obey their chiefs, and it is with the chiefs that the matter must be settled. I have already told these chiefs that you were not pleased with the way in which the work is being pushed through your lands. The Governor himself will come to meet you. He will listen to your griefs; he will propose a remedy. And if the compromise does not suit you, that will be the time to order the builders out of your reserve."

Crowfoot agreed. He'd already consulted with Lieutenant-Colonel A.G. Irvine, the Commissioner of the North West Mounted Police, and asked him if he thought he, Crowfoot, could stop the railway. Irvine replied by asking

Crowfoot if all the men in the world could stop the Bow River running.

The chief resigned himself to the inevitable. He didn't believe in foolhardy gestures. Not longer after, Dewdney arrived and agreed to give the Indians extra land in return for the railway's right of way.

CHAPTER EIGHT

The birth of Calgary

WILLIAM MURDOCH, A HARNESS-MAKER, put up the first commercial sign on the site of Calgary in May, 1883. To him, a newcomer from the East, the embryo town seemed like a distant planet. "I was dreaming about home almost all night," Murdoch wrote in his diary on a bitter, windy June day. "How I long to see my wife, mother, and little ones. My heart craves for them all today more than usual."

Murdoch would become the first mayor of this new city. But he couldn't get so much as a sliver of dressed lumber because there were no sawmills in the foothills. All that was available were rough planks – whipsawed vertically by hand. Fresh fruit was so scarce that when half a box of apples arrived they were sold at fifty cents each.

The settlement watched the railway approach with a mixture of worry and excitement. Where would the station be located? Under the terms of its contract, the CPR had title to the odd-numbered sections along the right of way. Fort Calgary and surrounding log structures, together with all the squatters' shacks, were situated on an even-numbered section – number 14 – on the east bank of the Elbow River near its junction with the Bow.

The neighbouring section, 15, on the opposite bank of the Elbow, had been reserved by Order-In-Council for the police horses to graze. So everyone figured the town would have to be put on the east bank where the fort was located.

On June 1, the giant scrapers lumbered through, tearing up the prairie soil. An army of graders followed close behind. The tension began to mount. The bridgers finished spanning the Bow on August 10. Two days later the first construction train puffed in. On August 15, a train carrying a temporary station arrived and the community held its breath.

Where would it stop? To everyone's surprise and dismay, it shunted directly through the settlement, crossed the new bridge, and stopped at a siding on Section 15 on the far side of the river.

The people living on the banks of the Elbow had no idea what to do. No survey had been taken. The ownership of Section 15 was in dispute. The town was growing rapidly on the east bank, but because everyone wanted to wait for the decision about the townsite, no one wanted to go to the expense of building anything permanent. And so, for all of 1883, Calgary was a tent city.

On August 20 two men arrived from the East, put up a tent and started to publish a newspaper, the *Herald*. Its first edition, dated August 31, said it would always have the courage of its convictions and wouldn't be afraid to speak its mind freely when wrongs had to be righted.

That same edition announced that, four days before, the leading directors of the CPR had come to Calgary aboard Van Horne's private car. They had made the trip from Winnipeg over the new track travelling at an average rate of more than thirty-five miles (56 km) an hour. At some points the locomotives, fed from recently discovered coal deposits near Medicine Hat, had pulled the cars at a clip of sixty miles (96 km) an hour.

The directors invited Father Lacombe, who had saved them from so much grief, to be their guest at luncheon. Then they voted to make Lacombe president of the CPR for one hour. Taking the chair, the priest immediately voted himself two passes on the railroad for life and, in addition, free transportation of all freight and baggage necessary to the Oblate missions, together with free use for himself for life of the CPR's telegraph system. The railway was only too happy to give him that because of what he had done.

All the promises made that day were honoured by the CPR. Lacombe used to lend out his passes to anyone who asked for them. And this too was tolerated. On one occasion, the two passes, which became familiar along the line, were presented by two nuns who had just arrived in the West. "May I ask," the conductor politely inquired, "which one is Father Lacombe?" But he let the blushing sisters go on their way.

After honouring the priest, the visitors left Calgary

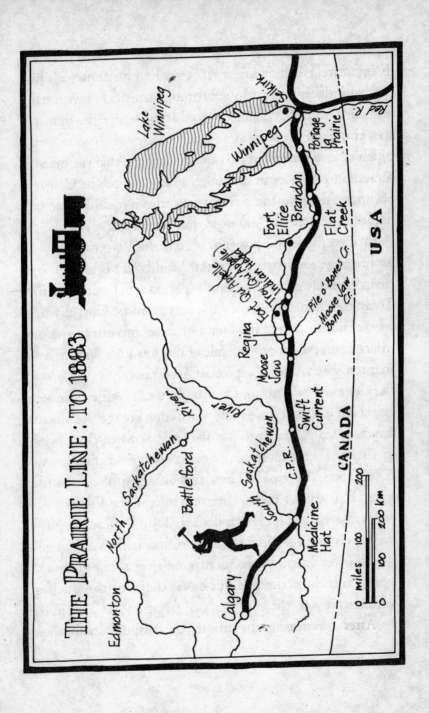

THE PRAIRIE LINE: TO 1883

Lake Winnipeg
Selkirk
Red R.
Winnipeg
Portage la Prairie
Brandon
Fort Ellice
Flat Creek
Fort Qu'Appelle
(Troy) (Qu'Appelle) (Indian Head)
Pile o' Bones Cr.
USA
Regina
Moose Jaw Bone Cr.
North Saskatchewan River
Moose Jaw
Battleford
Swift Current
C.P.R.
South Saskatchewan River
CANADA
Edmonton
Medicine Hat
Calgary

0 miles 100 200
0 100 200 km

without leaving the puzzled settlers any the wiser about their future. All they knew was they had no control. This state of indecision continued throughout the fall with half the community swearing it would not budge an inch to accommodate the railway.

The *Herald* continued to demand in vain that the matter be settled one way or the other. "The people in Calgary have by this time the elements of suspense and patience reduced to a science," it wrote that November.

In December the paper reported that "we have much pleasure in announcing that our friends east of the Elbow have definitely decided upon the permanent location of the city in that quarter. Already the surveyors are hard at work on the subdivision of the Denny Estate, and our next issue will contain the date of the sale of this beautiful spot so well adapted for the future capital of Alberta."

But the CPR itself and nobody else – editor, banker, merchant, or real estate man – would make the decision as to where Calgary was to be. In January, when the Order-In-Council regarding the police pasturage was finally cancelled, the CPR spoke. The city would not be on the east after all, it would be on the west side of the Elbow right where the station had been placed. To underline the point the government, which stood to profit equally with the railway, moved the post office across the river to the west.

In vain, the Denny subdivision on the east side advertised that it was "the centre of Calgary city." As soon as the post office crossed the river, James Bannerman followed with his flour and feed store. All the pledges about staying pat and refusing to follow the railway were forgotten. A wild scramble ensued as butcher shop, jeweller, churches, billiard parlour, and hotels packed up like gypsies and moved to the favoured site.

The *Herald* reported that buildings were suddenly springing up "as though some magical influence was being exerted," and that what had been barren prairie just three weeks before "is now rapidly growing into the shape of a respectable town."

Once again the railway, in truth "a magical influence," had set the pattern for the new Northwest. From Brandon to Calgary, the shape of the settled prairies was totally dictated by the CPR.

Index

England, 34

Coming Soon

TRAILS OF '98

There was no single trail to the fabled riches of the Yukon's Klondike region. There were many. And all of them were difficult.

In *Trails of '98,* Pierre Berton vividly captures all the determination and folly, courage and foolhardiness of the would-be prospectors who crossed ocean, mountain, river, and glacier in search of gold. Some men spent two years on these trails. Of the thousands who took them, the vast majority never reached the longed-for Klondike at all!

Trails of '98 is the third volume in a series devoted to the frenzy for gold that gripped Canada's Yukon – and the world – between 1896 and 1899.